LAZY VEGAN RECIPES

Learn to Cook Healthy Vegan Meals in No Time

Contents

INTRODUCTION 4

THE SHOPPING LIST OF A VEGAN COOKER 6

VEGAN EASY TO DO BREAKFAST 16

VEGAN LUNCH 24

GO FOR AN EASY VEGAN DINNER 46

DESSERT AND OTHER VEGAN GOODIES 56

GOOD TO KNOW 60

INTRODUCTION

Veganism is, in short, a lifestyle, where people exclude from their daily life any form of exploitation of animals (food or other products coming from animals. As for the eating habits, vegan people do not eat animal products, such as meat, fish, eggs, and milk from animals, honey, or any other derivate.

A quick list of products that veganism does not approve is, besides food:

- → **Clothes**: leather, silk, wool, skins from reptiles etc.;
- → **Decorations:** pearls, ivory, feathers;
- → **Cosmetics** made out of animal fats and oil; cosmetics tested on animals;
- → **Sports,** such as hunting or fishing;
- → **Entertainment**, such as zoos or circuses;
- → **Medical products:** vaccines or any other substances from animals;

Contemporary vegans also suggest that a vegan lifestyle provides benefits in terms of health, weight, and psychological balance. Moreover, veganism is thought to be a good way to protect the environment and the natural resources worldwide, water in particular.

The increasing benefits of veganism generated a worldwide movement towards it and an increasing respect for animals. More and more people choose a vegan lifestyle.

However, as we need to eat daily, I thought it would be easy to have at hand recipes that can be cooked fast, and with little effort. I do not necessarily advocate for fast cooking, but let's agree it is extremely helpful to have access to some recipes in the case of emergency.

THE SHOPPING LIST OF A VEGAN COOKER

The secret of any good recipe is the ingredients. Therefore, it is important to have close to you all the agreed elements of a vegan diet. I remember now how hard was for me at the beginning to shop like a vegan.

I had in mind a short list of rules that guided me in the process:

1. I always **eat before going shopping**; I am more confident and I have more energy to do the shopping without hurry; also, eating before helps me avoid buying any junk food that I do not actually need;

2. I **make the list from home, in writing;** I will give you details on what type of ingredients you will need to buy to make all the vegan recipes;

3. I **avoid walking in the store,** and not check for new products; it is very helpful to go directly in the sections I am interested in;

4. I **check the ingredients** of everything I buy; it is a rule that applies mostly in case of bread, as I want to be made by whole grain flour;

I provide below a table of most of the products that go extremely well on a vegan diet, split into categories of foods.

Product	Examples
VEGETABLES	Fresh: → Asparagus → Avocado → Bell peppers → Broccoli → Carrots → Cauliflower → Celery → Cucumbers → Garlic → Kale → Mushrooms → Onions (red, white, green) → Squashes → Sugar snap peas → Tomatoes → Zucchini
	Vegetables with green leaves: → Baby kale → Baby spinach → Butter lettuce → Leaf lettuce → Romaine → Salad mixes
	Frozen vegetables: → Asparagus → Broccoli → Corn → Edamame → Peas → Spinach → Stir-fry mixes

Keep in mind:

- be sure to have a good variety of vegetables in your fridge;
- be sure to buy different vegetables, frozen and/or fresh;
- frozen vegetables are more versatile;
- always include leafy green vegetables in your list;

Product	Examples
FRUITS	Fresh: → Apples → Apricots → Bananas → Blackberries → Blueberries → Cantaloupe → Cherries → Grapefruit → Grapes → Honeydew → Kiwis → Lemons → Limes → Mangoes → Nectarines → Oranges → Peaches → Pears → Plums → Raspberries → Strawberries → Watermelon Frozen fruits: → Blueberries → Mango

	→ Mixed berry blends → Mixed fruit blends → Raspberries → Strawberries → Sweet cherries
	Dried fruits: → Apple slices → Apricots → Banana chips → Cranberries → Currants → Dates → Figs → Raisins

Keep in mind
- buy fruits from different categories, so you can have a lot of options to choose from;
- you can choose between fresh, frozen or dried fruits; each of them goes well in different recipes;
- dried fruits are excellent as snacks or when you are in a hurry and cannot cook something very fancy;
- buy some fruits that are available throughout the whole season, and after that pick some fruits of the season;

Product	Examples

BEANS, GRAINS, AND GREENS	Products made of 100% whole grains: → Bagels → Bread → English muffins → Pasta → Pitas → Tortillas	
	Whole grains: → Brown rice → Oatmeal (quick, rolled, or steel-cut) → Quinoa → Russet potatoes → Seitan (gluten from wheat) → Sweet potatoes	
	Beans: → Black beans → Chickpeas → Hummus → Kidney beans → Lentils → Veggie burgers (lentil, bean, or vegetable based) *you can take the beans canned or dry;	
	Products made of soy: → Edamame → Soy milk → Tempeh → Tofu	

Keep in mind
- buy at least 2 products made of 100% whole grains; they are very good for sandwiches or to go lunches; you can easily freeze them;
- oatmeal is a must have in this category; however, avoid any oatmeal packages that are precooked; I suggest you look for rolled or steel-cut oats;

Product	Examples
FATS	→ Almond/Nut butter → Almonds → Avocado → Canola oil → Cashews → Chia seeds → Coconut milk → Coconut oil → Dark chocolate → Earth Balance butter → Edamame → Flax seed oil → Ground flax seeds → Hummus → Olive oil → Olives → Peanut butter → Pecans → Pumpkin seeds → Sesame oil → Sesame seeds → Sunflower seed butter → Sunflower seeds → Tahini (sesame butter) → Walnuts

Keep in mind
- healthy fats are very necessary in everyone's diet; in cases of vegan diets, healthy fats can be taken from a lot of other foods;
- a good source of healthy fats are the whole foods, such as avocado, nuts, or olives;
- some oils also provide the needed quantity of healthy fats;
- keep nuts or seed in the freezer, to keep them fresh;

Product	Examples
PLANT BASED MILK PRODUCTS	Milk: → Almond milk → Coconut milk → Flax milk → Hemp milk → Oat milk → Rice milk → Soy milk
	Yogurt: → Almond yogurt → Coconut yogurt → Soy yogurt
Keep in mind: - choose products that are not sweetened; this way you can use them not only for dessert but in many other recipes; - soy milk is very high in protein;	

Product	Examples
CONDIMENTS, HERBS, AND SPICES	Sweeteners: → Agave syrup → Coconut sugar → Dark chocolate chips → Dates → Dried fruits → Fruit preserves → Maple syrup → Molasses → Organic cane sugar → Stevia
	Herbs: → Basil → Chili powder → Cinnamon → Cumin → Oregano → Pepper → Salt → Thyme → Turmeric
	Condiments: → Hummus → Lemon/lime juice → Mustard → Nutritional yeast → Salsa → Soy sauce

	→ Vegan mayo
	→ Vegetable bouillon
	→ Vinegar (white, balsamic)
	For cooking/baking:
	→ Apple cider vinegar
	→ Baking powder
	→ Baking soda
	→ Cocoa
	→ Coconut oil
	→ Corn starch
	→ Earth Balance Butter
	→ Ground flax seed
	→ Whole grain flour
	→ Yeast
Keep in mind: - you will need a very good selection of herbs and spices because they make it very easy to savour your meals; - be sure to have close two-three types of sweeteners; I have one to sweeten my coffee, another for oatmeal and a different sweetener for baking;	

The above-mentioned lists help you in doing the shopping in order to cook most of the vegan recipes you will find here or elsewhere. Besides these, you can find some vegan alternatives, full of protein and other nutrients. The alternatives are most of the times tasty and easy to cook. Their use is highly appreciated when people go from a meat-based diet to a vegan diet, but I do not recommend these on a long-term basis.

The purpose of the vegan alternatives is to replace the traditional burgers, pizza, and hotdogs with some vegan versions. Because these substitutes are highly processed, I recommend you eat them in moderation and for a very short period of time.

However, you can find on the market some products that are minimally processed and can be consumed with less worry:

- → Bean or lentil burgers
- → Earth Balance butter
- → Marinated tempeh bacon
- → Marinated tofu
- → Nutritional yeast
- → Plain non-dairy yogurts
- → Plant-based milks
- → Plant-based yogurts
- → Seitan
- → Soy cheese
- → Soy coffee creamers
- → Tempeh bacon
- → Textured vegetable protein
- → Unsweetened plant milk
- → Veggie or soy burgers
- → Veggie or soy hot dogs
- → Veggie sausages

VEGAN EASY TO DO BREAKFAST

When I got employed, I had a schedule that implied waking up extremely early, somewhere around 6 a.m. Because I am a person that likes sleeping a lot, I skipped breakfast as many times as I could.

After a few years of functioning like that, my body showed signs of tiredness and irritation all day long. Something changed when I decided to switch to a vegan way of life. Together with this, I changed my perspective on the importance of breakfast.

I began preparing healthy and nutritionally breakfasts every day. This assured me a better concentration at work, more strength and the ability to focus all day long. Finally, the surprise was that I also had lower levels of cholesterol.

Below, I put together a list of my favorite recipes for breakfast, for a healthy vegan diet every day. I am well aware that you can find a lot more, but these are the ones I like most and I hope you will enjoy them as much as I do.

1. **Oatmeal cake and coconut cream**

Ingredients (for 1 person):

For Oatmeal Cake:

- ½ cup water
- ½ cup soy or almond milk
- ¼ tsp. vanilla
- 1 tbsp. raisins
- ½ cup of oats
- 1 medium carrot, grated
- 1 ½ tbsp. of walnuts (chopped)
- ½ tbsp. maple syrup
- cinnamon and ground ginger (1/8 tsp. of each)

For the coconut cream:

- High-quality coconut cream, 1 spoon (it is best if it is chilled; be sure to be a brand that has the highest percentage of coconut; I recommend the canned coconut cream)

Additional: you can add chopped pecans, raisins, or/and grated carrots.

Instructions:

- put the water, the soy milk, and the vanilla in a small saucepan, and heat it over medium;

- when the mixture begins to boil, add the raisins and let it boil for about 1 minute;

- add the oats, the carrot (grated), the ginger, and the walnuts; cook it for 5-8 minutes (until it gets almost thick); now you can add the cinnamon; sweeten with maple syrup; stir gently;

- mix the coconut cream from the can, until it softens; you can sweeten it with maple syrup if you like;

- serve the oatmeal cake in a bowl, with coconut cream topping; I also like to add some chopped pecans in a thin layer;

Time needed: 5 minutes to prepare and 10 minutes to cook.

2. Vegan pancakes

Ingredients (6-7 pancakes):

- → ½ cup whole wheat flour sifted;
- → 1 ½ tbsp. baking powder
- → 1/8 tsp. of salt;
- → 1 tsp vanilla
- → 1 cup of milk (soy or almond)
- → 1 tbsp. of coconut oil (melted)
- → 1 tbsp. of cane sugar (I like the organic type; you can add an extra tbsp. if you want it to be sweeter)

Instructions:

- Mix the dry ingredients in a bowl; use a whisk/mixer to combine the vanilla, the milk, the coconut oil and the sugar in another bowl;

- Add the liquid ingredients to the dry ones; mix them for 20-30 seconds; let the mixture for pancakes rest, while you heat a frying pan (recommended to be a non-stick pan) over the medium heat;

- Cook one pancake at a time; ¼ of the mixture should be enough for one piece; cook each side for 1-2 minutes;

Time needed: 10 minutes to prepare, 10-15 minutes to cook

3. Apple and oatmeal bowl

Ingredients (for 2 persons)

- → 2 tsp. of coconut oil
- → half of one small apple, chopped;
- → 2 tbsp. of pecans (chopped);
- → ¼ tsp. of cinnamon;
- → 2 cups of water;
- → 1 cup of flaked oats;
- → 1/8 tsp. of salt;
- → 1 tbsp. of flax seeds;
- → 2 tbsp. of raisins;
- → brown sugar (1 tbsp. or more, it depends on how sweet do you want it to be);
- → almond milk
- → any toppings you like (apple slices, pumpkin seeds);

Instructions:

- use a small saucepan to heat the coconut oil, in which you add the apple and bake it for 1-2 minutes;

- add the chopped pecans and the cinnamon, and cook for one minute; add the water and boil the mixture;

- put the flake oats and the salt; boil at a medium heat, until the oats thickens;

- add the flax seeds, the raisins, the brown sugar and just a little bit of the almond milk; boil until it becomes thick;

- put it in a bowl and add the topping you like (almond milk, pecans, raisins, brown sugar, some apple slices).

Time needed: 5 minutes to prepare, 10 minutes to cook.

4. Green smoothie

Ingredients (for 2 persons)

- → 1 cup milk (soy or almond)
- → spinach (2 handfuls)
- → 2 bananas (frozen, but not necessarily)
- → pitted date fruits (4-5 pieces)
- → 2 tbsp. of hemp
- → 1 tbsp. peanut butter
- → 2-3 ice cubes

For the topping (it is optional)
- → hemp seeds;
- → chia seeds
- → pumpkin seeds
- → almonds

*2 tbsp. of each

Instructions:

- mix all the ingredients in a blender, until it is smooth;

- blend the ingredients for the topping separately;

Time needed: 5 minutes to prepare

5. Green smoothie 2

Ingredients (for 1 person)

- → 1 cup almond milk (or any type of vegan milk, such as rice milk, soy milk, hemp milk, coconut milk);
- → 1 banana;
- → ½ cup of mango (chopped)
- → spinach (1-2 handfuls)
- → ¼ pumpkin seeds
- → 2 tbsp. of hemp hearts;
- → (optional) ½ tsp. of vanilla powder and 2 tsp. of water

Instructions:

- Put in a blender first the spinach, the banana, and the seeds;
- Add the milk and mix it until the seeds are smooth;

Time needed: 5 minutes to prepare

Nutrients:

Almond milk: a very good source of vitamin E and calcium;
Banana: vitamin B6, potassium, vitamin C;
Mango: vitamin C, vitamin A, potassium;
Spinach: vitamin K, vitamin C, vitamin A;
Pumpkin seeds: protein, iron, magnesium, potassium;
Hemp hearts: protein, essential fat acids;

6. Scrambled Tofu

Ingredients (for 1 person)

- → ½ piece of a firm or pressed tofu
- → ½ tbsp. olive oil
- → 1 clove garlic, chopped
- → 1 tbsp. of nutritional yeast
- → 1/8 tsp. cumin (ground)
- → 1/8 tsp salt

Instructions:

- Use a frying pan to heat the olive oil (sometimes I use coconut oil); break the piece of tofu into large chunks;

- When the pan is heated over medium high, put the tofu and the garlic in the oil;

- Cook it until the tofu gets golden on every side; use a wooden spoon;

- When the tofu is cooked, add the yeast, cumin, and the salt; cook it until the tofu takes in the yeast;

- Serve it with toast, or fresh fruit; I also like scrambled tofu with whole wheat bread, with non-dairy cheese, or with lettuce and tomato.

Time needed: 5 minutes to prepare, 10 minutes to cook

VEGAN LUNCH

Working on a full-time basis allowed me a little break for lunch. When I went to a vegan lifestyle, I also changed my job. As a freelancer, I can take the time to cook for lunch. However, if you have a work that does not allow you cooking, you can easily prepare the lunch at home. Let me tell you some of my most dear easy to do recipes.

1. **Vegan sandwich**

You can practically make any kind of sandwich you like. My favorite sandwich includes the following ingredients:

Ingredients (for 1 sandwich)

- → 2 slices of bread (whole wheat)
- → 2 tsp. vegan mayo
- → 2 tsp. tomato sauce (I use homemade tomato sauce)
- → 1-2 slices of vegan cheese;
- → Fresh cucumber and lettuce;
- → Oregano and basil (1/8 tsp.)

Instructions:
- on one slice of bread apply mayonnaise, add the cheese, the spices, the sliced cucumber and the lettuce;
- on the other slice of bread apply the tomato sauce and the spices;
- use a sandwich maker to make it crunchy and combine the two slices;

Time needed: 5 minutes to prepare

2. Potatoes, tofu, and green beans

Ingredients (for 2 persons)

→ 5 medium sized potatoes
→ 100 g green beans
→ ½ medium onion (chopped)
→ ½ medium carrot
→ A pinch of chopped dill
→ 1/8 tsp. of salt
→ 5 tbsp. of olive oil (or any vegetable oil you like)
→ 1-2 cups of water

Instructions:

- Chop all the ingredients;

- Heat the oil in a saucepan; put the potatoes first and cook them for about 5 minutes; add beans, carrot, and onions, and cook for about 5 more minutes;

- Add the water and boil for 10 more minutes; from time to time stir and if necessary, add some more water so the vegetables get stewed enough;

- Add the spices and the tofu (chopped in cubes), cook for no more than a minute; mix everything and let it rest a couple of minutes, so all the flavors get together;

Time needed: 20 minutes to prepare, 20-30 minutes to cook

3. Tomato pasta and garlic toast

Ingredients (for 2 persons)

For tomato sauce

- → 2 tomatoes (chopped)
- → 2 cloves garlic (minced)
- → ½ tbsp. olive oil
- → ¼ tsp. oregano
- → 1/8 tsp. thyme
- → a pinch of salt
- → 1 cup of vegetable soup (you can also use warm water)

For garlic toast

- → ¼ cup of vegan butter;
- → 2 cloves garlic
- → Whole wheat bread (a French baguette or a sliced loaf)

Instructions:

- Put together the tomatoes, garlic, olive oil, oregano, thyme, and salt; put them on a baking sheet, in a baking pan and roast them in the preheated oven for 15-20 minutes;
- Move the tomatoes in a saucepan, add the vegetable soup (or 1 cup of warm water) and boil it for another 10 minutes; let them simmer until they get to a consistency you like;
- For the garlic toast, combine the butter with the garlic; spread the mixture on the sliced bread;

- In a large frying pan, that was previously heated, put the slices of bread, with the garlic butter side down; cook them for 4-5 minutes, until they get a golden color; turn the slices and warm the side with no butter for 1 minute;
- Serve the garlic toast with the tomato sauce;

4. Asparagus and peas with Alfredo sauce

Ingredients (for 2 persons)

For Asparagus & Peas
- 1/2 box of noodles (or any pasta you like; fettuccine noodles go the best)
- ½ tbsp. olive oil
- ½ cup of asparagus (cut into log pieces)
- 1 clove garlic (minced)
- ½ peas (frozen, prepared)

For Alfredo Sauce
- 2-3 cups of cauliflower
- 2 cloves garlic (minced)
- 1 tbsp. olive oil
- 1 cup of vegetable soup (or 1 cup of warm water)
- ½ cup almond milk
- 1 tbsp. yeast
- a pinch of salt and black pepper

Instructions:

Alfredo Sauce
- boil water in a large pot, with a pinch of salt; add the cauliflower and cook them for around 10 minutes; drain the cauliflower and put it aside;
- boil the pasta in a pot of water with a little salt;
- in a frying pan (skillet), put the olive oil, heat it, add the garlic and cook it until it becomes translucent;
- combine the cauliflower, the cooked garlic, the olive oil half of the vegetable soup (broth), and the yeast; add salt and pepper and mix it until it is creamy; use the rest of the vegetable soup to adjust the sauce consistency; put aside the sauce;

- once you cooked the pasta, do not cook them; mix the boiled pasta with the Alfredo sauce while the pasta is still hot;

Final serving
- in a frying pan, heat a splash of olive oil; add the asparagus and the garlic, and cook the asparagus until it is soft; add peas, salt, and pepper;
- combine the pasta (with the Alfredo sauce added) with the vegetables (asparagus and peas) and on top add whatever fresh herbs you like;

Time needed: 15 minutes to prepare, 20 minutes to cook

5. Tomato salad with tofu

Ingredients (for 2 persons)

For the salad:

- → 5 handfuls baby spinach
- → 15 medium tomatoes, cut in half
- → 10 leaves of sliced basil
- → 4 tbsp. balsamic vinaigrette
- → ½ avocado
- → 4 tbsp. pumpkin seeds

Soy Sauce Tofu
- → 2 pieces of tofu
- → 1 tsp. olive oil
- → 4 tbsp. soy sauce
- → 3 tbsp. Sriracha sauce[1]

Instructions:
- Put together the tomatoes, with the basil and the balsamic vinaigrette; let them marinate while you prepare the tofu (use half of the marinade);
- Preheat the oven at a medium heat level;
- Slice the tofu the shape you want;
- Mix gently the sliced tofu with olive oil, Sriracha sauce and soy sauce; spread the mix on a baking sheet, in a baking pan and cook it in the oven for around 10 minutes;
- Flip the tofu on the other side put the other half of the marinade and bake for another 10 minutes;

---

[1] A type of hot chili sauce made of chili peppers, vinegar, garlic, sugar, and salt. It comes from Thailand.

- When the tofu got crispy on both sides, take them from the oven;
- Serve the prepared tofu with spinach, the tomatoes, soy sauce tofu, avocado (chopped) and pumpkin seeds;

Time needed: 15 minutes to prepare, 20 minutes to cook

6. Potato salad

Ingredients (for 2 persons)

- 3 medium-large potatoes, peeled and sliced in four
- 2 tbsp. vegan mayo
- 1 tbsp. juice from pickles (or lemon juice)
- a pinch of salt
- ½ tsp. paprika
- black pepper
- 1 medium carrot, chopped
- ¼ of a medium celery, chopped
- 1 tbsp. dill, also chopped
- 1 small onion, chopped (preferably red, and put in cold water for 10 minutes)
- 1 small green bell pepper, chopped
- 1 small red bell pepper, chopped

Instructions:

- Boil the potatoes, in a large pot, with a pinch of salt; cook until they are tender, and avoid overcooking;
- In a bowl, combine the vegan mayo, the pickle juice (or the lemon), add paprika, salt, and black pepper; put these over the potatoes (drained from water when they are boiled); mash the potatoes with the dressing, slightly, with a fork; let it cool down;
- When the potatoes are cooled, add the carrot, the celery, the dill, the red onion, the bell peppers;
- Add any seasoning, as you like;
- Keep it in a fridge for at least half an hour before eating; the flavor combine great in this time;

Time needed: 20 minutes to prepare, 15 minutes to cook

7. Apple and almond butter sandwich

Ingredients (for 1 person)

- → 2 slice of bread (whole grain preferably)
- → 2 tbsp. almond butter
- → 1 medium apple, sliced
- → Cinnamon
- → Maple syrup/agave syrup

Instructions:

- Preheat the oven at a medium level;

- On each slice of bread spread a thick layer of almond butter;

- Put the slices of apple on each side, add cinnamon and a sprinkle of maple/agave syrup;

- Put the slices in the broiler, in the oven, for about 3 minutes; when the apple slices look tender, take them from the oven;

- Make the sandwich with the both slices and put it back in the oven for another 3 minutes; toast it on each side;

- Enjoy it while it is still hot.

Time needed: 10 minutes to prepare, 10 minutes to cook

8. Tofu sandwich

Ingredients (for 2 persons)

- → 1 piece of tofu
- → 3 medium sized onions (yellow or red), julienned
- → Whole grain bread (4 slices)
- → 1 tbsp. mustard
- → 1 avocado
- → 2 -3 leaves lettuce,
- → 1 tomato
- → 2 tsp of oil
- → 2 cloves garlic (minced)
- → 1 tbsp. soy sauce
- → 1 tbsp. maple syrup
- → ¼ tsp. liquid smoke[2]
- → 1 tbsp. water

Instructions:

- Marinate the tofu in the mix made from garlic, soy sauce, maple syrup, liquid smoke, and water (for 30 minutes to 1 hour;

- Put the onions in a frying pan and caramelize them at a low-level heat, for around 15 minutes; stir frequently and add water if necessary (so the onions do not dry out)

- Put the sliced tofu in the pan where you caramelized the onions and cook them at an over medium heat; cook them until they get brown on both sides;

---

[2] It is a liquid soluble in water, with colors from yellow to red; used for flavoring; also known as wood vinegar;

- Toast the bread; spread on one slice mustard, on the other slice a layer of mashed avocado; over the avocado add lettuce, tomato, the caramelized onion and the cooked tofu; put on top the slice with mustard; cut in two and enjoy.

Time needed: 15 minutes to prepare, 30 minutes to cook

9. Zucchini "Meatballs"

Ingredients (for around 12 "meatballs")

→ approximately 400 grams (1 can) chickpeas (drain and rinse them before you cook)
→ 3 cloves garlic
→ ½ cup rolled oats
→ 1 tsp. basil (dried)
→ 1 tsp. oregano (dried)
→ a pinch of salt;
→ 2 tbsp. yeast;
→ Juice from half of lemon
→ 1 large zucchini (or 2 smaller ones) shredded
→ 1 liter of Marinara sauce[3]
→ 200 grams of pasta, whole grain

Instructions:

- Mix chickpeas, the garlic, and oats; put them in a large bowl and add dried herbs, salt, yeast, lemon juice and zucchini; Mix them until are well-combined; it the mixture is too wet, add some extra oats or yeast;

- Preheat the oven; scoop out with a tablespoon of the zucchini mixture and roll separate balls; put them on a baking paper, in a pan; put the balls some cm apart; cook the "meatballs" for about 20 minutes;

- Meanwhile, boil the pasta in a pot of water, with a pinch of salt;

- Serve the meatballs with the pasta and Marinara sauce.

Time needed: 20 minutes to prepare, 25 minutes to cook

---

[3] An Italian sauce made from tomatoes, garlic, herbs, and onions.

10. Vegan Stew

Ingredients (for 4 persons)

- → 2 tbsp. olive oil
- → 1 onion, diced
- → 1 leek (remove the dark green part; slice the white part)
- → 2 cloves garlic, minced
- → 4 medium sized potatoes, peeled and chopped
- → 1 cup cooked beans (white beans go the best)
- → ½ cup green lentils (rinse and drain before you cook)
- → ½ tsp. oregano and thyme (dried)
- → 1 can peeled tomatoes
- → 3 cups water
- → a pinch of salt
- → a pinch of pepper
- → 4 stalks kale, chopped

Instructions:

- In a heavy bottomed pot, heat the oil; add onion and leek and cook until they are soft; add garlic and stir; cook for a minute or two

- Add potatoes, beans, lentils and herbs; combine them with a wooden spoon;

- Add tomatoes and water; boil; cook until the potatoes get soft (about 20 minutes); Add the kale, and cook for another 10 minutes; if there is too much water, you can boil some extra time;

Time needed: 20 minutes to prepare, 30 minutes to cook

11. Vegan chili

Ingredients (for 3 persons)

- → 1 tbsp. olive oil
- → ½ onion (white or yellow), chopped;
- → 1 red pepper, chopped;
- → 1 clove garlic, minced
- → 1 tbsp. chili powder
- → 1 tsp cumin
- → 1 tsp oregano (dried)
- → ½ tsp cinnamon
- → 2 cans peeled tomatoes
- → 1 can cooked lentils
- → 1 can cooked kidney beans
- → 1 can corn (drain and rinse before you cook)
- → a pinch of salt and a pinch of pepper

Instructions:

- heat the oil in a large pot and add the onion; cook it for about 3 minutes, until it is soft; add the red pepper and cook for another minute;
- add all the spices and stir; add the garlic and stir again to combine; add half of the tomatoes and cook for two more minutes;
- add the remaining ingredients (tomatoes, lentils, kidney beans, corn, salt, and pepper), stir and simmer for another 20 minutes;

Time needed: 15 minutes to prepare, 30 minutes to cook

12. Vegan Mac and Cheese

Ingredients (for 3 persons)

- → 1 medium sized carrot (diced)
- → ¼ onion (yellow or red, diced)
- → 200 grams canned white beans (drain and rinse before cooking)
- → ¼ cup cashews
- → ¼ tsp. garlic powder
- → a pinch of salt
- → 1 cup pasta (uncooked)

Instructions:

- Boil the pasta in a large pot, add the boiling water a pinch of salt;
- In another pot, boil around 1 cup of water, with the carrots and the onion (around 10 minutes); keep the water;
- Drain the cooked pasta in a large bowl (glass or ceramic);
- Use a blender/ a food processor or a mixer to combine cooked carrots, onion, beans, one cup of the water in which you boiled the carrots and the onion, cashews, garlic powder and salt; mix it until it is creamy; it should look like a soft cheese;
- Combine the mix with the pasta, while they are both still hot;

Time needed: 10 minutes to prepare, 15 minutes to cook

13. Tomato soup

Ingredients (for 2 persons)

- → 1 medium sized onion (white or yellow) chopped
- → ½ tbsp. vegan butter
- → 1 clove garlic, minced
- → ½ tbsp. tomato sauce
- → 2 medium sized tomatoes, chopped
- → ¼ can cashew cream
- → ½ tbsp. coconut sugar
- → a pinch of salt
- → a pinch of pepper

Instructions:

- use a pot to cook for 2-3 minutes the onion, in vegan butter; the onion should get soft; add garlic and cook for 2 more minutes; low the heat if needed, to avoid the garlic and onion to burn;
- add tomato sauce and stir for two more minutes; add a cup of water, the chopped tomatoes and boil; after that lower the heat and let it simmer;
- add cashew cream, coconut sugar, salt, and pepper; boil it for 20 minutes;

***how to make cashew cream: put raw cashew in water for at least 3 hours (or let them overnight); drain and rinse the cashews; blend them with water until it is creamy;

Time needed: 10 minutes to prepare, 30 minutes to cook

14. Potato and leek soup

Ingredients (for 3 persons)

- → 4-5 medium sized potatoes (peeled)
- → 1 tbsp. olive oil (or vegan butter)
- → 1 clove garlic, minced
- → 1 leek (cleaned, remove the dark green leaves), sliced
- → 2 cups vegetable soup (or warm water)
- → ½ tbsp. white miso[4], combined 1ith 1 tbsp. hot water (until it is a paste)
- → 3 tbsp. coconut cream
- → salt and pepper

Instructions:

- boil the potatoes in a pot with water and a pinch of salt; cook until the potatoes are tender; chop one boiled potato and leave the rest whole;

- use a large saucepan to heat the oil; add leeks, garlic, salt, and pepper; cook until they are soft; leave half of the leek aside;

- add the whole potatoes, the vegetable soup (or the warm water); purée the soup with a mixer; add the chopped potatoes and the remaining leeks and let to boil; when the soup is boiled, add the coconut cream and the miso soup; stir for a couple of minutes; adjust the taste with salt/pepper;

---

[4] traditional Japanese seasoning; it is produced from fermented soybeans with salt and koji, rice, barley and other ingredients; it is a thick paste; used for sauces, pickling vegetables or meats; usually it is salty;

Time needed: 20 minutes to prepare, 20 minutes to cook

15. Broccoli Soup

Ingredients (for 3 persons)

For the broccoli soup:

- → 2 tbsp. olive oil
- → 3 cups broccoli, chopped
- → 1 small carrot, chopped
- → ¼ celery, chopped
- → 1 small onion (yellow or white) chopped
- → 1 clove garlic, minced
- → a pinch of salt
- → 3 tbsp. whole wheat flour
- → 1 cup almond or soy milk, unsweetened
- → ¼ cup coconut milk
- → 1 tsp. yeast

For Broccoli "Croutons"
- → 5 broccoli stalks
- → 2 tsp. olive oil

Instructions:

The broccoli soup
- Take a medium saucepan; heat the olive oil; add broccoli, carrot, celery, onion, garlic and salt; cook until the onion is tender;
- Add flour and cook for at least 1 minute; pour in the vegetable soup; the soup gets thicker as you boil; add the milk and the yeast;
- Boil at a medium-low heat for about 10 minutes (the vegetables need to get tender); Purée the soup;

The broccoli "Croutons"
- In a small pan heat the olive oil, add broccoli and a pinch of salt; cook until it is soft;
- Cook for another 5 minutes at a high heat level, until the broccoli gets a brown edge;

- Serve the soup with the broccoli florets;

Time needed: 20 minutes to prepare, 30 minutes to cook

16. Potato and asparagus soup

Ingredients (for 2 persons)

- → ½ tbsp. olive oil
- → ¼ medium red onion, chopped
- → ¼ medium celery, chopped
- → 1 small carrot, chopped
- → 1 clove garlic, minced
- → 1 cup chopped asparagus
- → 3 medium potatoes
- → a pinch of salt
- → ¼ tbsp. whole wheat flour
- → 1 ½ cups vegetable soup (or warm water)
- → 1 cup vegan cheese
- → 1 tbsp. yeast
- → ½ cup almond/soy milk

Instructions:

- Use a saucepan to heat the oil; put onion, celery, carrot, garlic, asparagus, potatoes, and salt; cook for 5 minutes;

- Add flour, stir, cook for one more minute;

- Add vegetable soup (or warm water), turn the heat up; boil for 20 minutes (until the potatoes are tender)

- purée the soup; add vegan cheese and yeast; turn the heat down and boil until the cheese is melted; add the milk and stir;

Time needed: 15 minutes to prepare, 30 minutes to cook

17. Mushroom soup

Ingredients (for 2 persons)

→ 1 tbsp. coconut oil/olive oil
→ 1 small onion, diced (white or yellow)
→ 5 cups diced mushrooms (cremini goes the best)
→ 2 cloves garlic, minced
→ 1 tsp. thyme (fresh)
→ ½ cup dry white wine
→ 1 cup coconut milk (the full-fat version)
→ 2 cups vegetable soup (or warm water)
→ 1 tsp. salt
→ ½ tsp pepper
→ 6 handfuls baby spinach

Instructions:

- Heat the oil in a large pot; add onion and cook for 2-3 minutes, until it is soft; add the mushrooms and cook for another 5 minutes;

- When the mushrooms begin to release water, add garlic and thyme, and cook for 3 minutes; low the heat to prevent the garlic from burning;

- When most of the water released by mushrooms is absorbed, add white wine and boil for 5 more minutes;

- Add coconut milk, vegetable soup, salt, and pepper; stir and let it boil for about 20 minutes; before you turn off the heat add the spinach;

Time needed: 10 minutes to prepare, 35 minutes to cook

GO FOR AN EASY VEGAN DINNER

1. Tofu and brown rice

Ingredients (for 2 persons)

- → ½ piece of tofu, chopped
- → 2 tsp. olive oil
- → ½ small red onion, sliced
- → ½ cup kale, chopped
- → 1 medium carrot, chopped
- → ½ green/red bell pepper, chopped
- → 1 small zucchini, sliced
- → ½ cup mushrooms, sliced
- → 1 clove garlic, minced
- → 1/6 tsp. cumin
- → ¼ tsp. coriander
- → ¼ tsp. turmeric
- → ¼ tsp. salt
- → 1 cup vegetable soup (or warm water)
- → ½ cup coconut milk
- → 1/6 cup fresh basil, chopped
- → juice from ¼ lemon
- → 2 cups brown rice, cooked

Instructions:
- Use a sauce pan to heat 2 tsp. oil; cook the tofu until it gets evenly brown; put aside the cooked tofu

- In the same pan, add 1 tsp oil, the onion, and vegetables (except kale); cook them until they are soft and then put aside;
- Continue in the same saucepan; add another tsp. of oil, garlic, cumin, coriander, and salt; cook one minute, until the garlic is translucent; add the vegetables soup, coconut milk, and kale, the vegetables and the tofu you put aside earlier; cook for another 5-10 minutes;
- When the curry has boiled, add lemon juice and basil; adjust the seasoning
- Serve it with brown rice.

Time needed: 20 minutes to prepare, 25 minutes to cook

2. Potato and broccoli bowl

Ingredients (for 4 persons)

For Béchamel Sauce

- → 1 tsp vegan butter
- → 1 tsp whole wheat flour
- → ½ small onion (red), finely chopped
- → ¼ tsp. garlic powder
- → 1/8 tsp. turmeric
- → 1/8 tsp. paprika
- → a pinch of salt
- → ½ vegetable soup
- → 1 cup soy milk
- → 1/6 cup yeast flakes
- → 1/6 cup vegan cheese

Potato and Broccoli bowl

- → 5 medium sized potatoes
- → 6-7 florets of broccoli, sliced;
- → ½ cup bread crumbs
- → ½ tbsp. vegan butter/olive oil
- → 1/8 tsp. (a pinch) garlic powder
- → 1/8 tsp. onion powder
- → 1/8 tsp. oregano
- → Salt and pepper, to taste

Instructions:
The Béchamel Sauce

- Heat in a saucepan 2 tbsp. of vegan butter, add red onion, cook until is translucent; add the flour, garlic powder, turmeric, paprika, salt; whisk and cook for 1 minute;

- Slowly add the vegetable soup and the soy milk (unsweetened), followed by the yeast and the cheese; turn the heat down and boil until the cheese is melted (for a few minutes);

The Potato and Broccoli bowl

- Preheat the oven at a medium level;

- Put together bread crumbs, melted butter, garlic powder, onion powder, oregano, and salt;

- Use a pie plate; spread oil in a thin layer on the plate's bottom; add 1 layer of sliced potatoes; add another thin layer of Béchamel Sauce and a layer of broccoli; repeat, until you finish the potatoes and the broccoli; the top layer should be sauce and bread crumbs;

- Bake it covered (with aluminium foil) for 50 minutes and another 10 minutes uncovered.

Time needed: 45 minutes to prepare, 60 minutes to cook

***even if it is a recipe that takes time, I chose it because it can be prepared for dinner and for the lunch next day;

3. Nacho Plate

Ingredients (for 2 persons)

→ 1 bag of tortilla chips (app. 250 grams)
→ ½ cup chopped tomatoes
→ 1 green bell pepper, chopped
→ 1 small red onion, chopped
→ 5 black olives, sliced
→ ¼ cup kidney beans

To serve
→ ½ iceberg lettuce, shredded
→ 2 small tomatoes, chopped
→ 1 handful cilantro, chopped
→ ½ cup guacamole[5]
→ ½ cup hummus

Instructions:
- Preheat the oven at a medium level;
- Put the chips in a baking tray, on a sheet of baking paper; add the tomato, green pepper, onion, olives, beans;
- Bake for 5-10 minutes (until all the ingredients are crispy)
- Top with iceberg lettuce and cilantro; serve with guacamole and hummus

---

[5] A sauce made from mashed ripe avocados and salt; some recipes include tomato, onion, and garlic;

Time needed: 20 minutes to prepare, 10 minutes to cook

4. Pesto Sauce and Potatoes

Ingredients (for 2 persons)

For the pesto sauce

- → 1 handful basil leaves
- → ¼ cup cashews
- → 1 clove garlic
- → a pinch of salt
- → ½ tsp miso
- → 2 tbsp. yeast
- → 2 tbsp. hemp seeds
- → 3 tbsp. olive oil
- → 3 tbsp. water

For roasted potatoes

- → 6 medium sized potatoes
- → 1 tbsp. olive oil
- → salt

Instructions:

For the pesto sauce

- mix in a blender or a food processor basil, cashews, garlic, salt; mix it until it has a creamy texture;

- add miso, yeast and hemp seeds; combine them evenly; put the sauce in a ceramic/glass bowl and cover with a thin layer of olive oil so it does not oxidize;

For the roasted potatoes

- Preheat the oven at a medium level;

- Cut the potatoes in half;

- Put in a baking a pan the potatoes, with olive oil and salt; mix well and spread in the tray; bake on each side for about 15 minutes;

Time needed: 10 minutes to prepare, 30 minutes to cook

5. Roasted vegetables

Ingredients (for 2 persons)

Potatoes and Chickpeas
- → 6 medium potatoes, peeled and cut in four
- → 1 can chickpeas (drain and rinse before cooking)
- → 2 tsp. olive oil
- → 1 tbsp. Sriracha sauce
- → garlic and onion powder (1/2 tsp of each)
- → ½ tsp turmeric
- → a pinch of salt

Roasted Carrots
- → 2 medium carrots, sliced
- → 1 tsp. olive oil
- → 1 tsp. maple syrup
- → ¼ tsp. garlic (powder)
- → ½ tsp. turmeric
- → ¼ tsp. paprika
- → a pinch of salt

Zucchini
- → 1 medium zucchini, sliced
- → 1 tsp. olive oil
- → salt and pepper to taste

Kale
- → 1 hand of kale, chopped
- → 1 tsp. olive oil
- → 1 clove garlic, minced
- → Lemon juice from ½ lemon
- → salt and pepper to taste

Hummus
- → 1 tbsp. hummus
- → 1 tbsp. tahini
- → 2 tbsp. water
- → 2 tsp lemon juice
- → ½ tsp garlic powder
- → 1 tbsp. yeast
- → 1 tsp olive oil
- → salt, to taste

Instructions:
The roasted vegetables

- Potatoes and chickpeas: preheat the oven at a medium level; combine all the ingredients in a bowl, and move them in a baking pan;

- Roasted carrots: combine all the ingredients (carrots, olive oil, garlic powder, turmeric, paprika, maple syrup and salt) and add them to the potatoes and chickpeas;

- Zucchini: combine all the ingredients and add them in the baking pan, together with the potatoes, chickpeas, and carrots;

- Bake all of these for about 15 minutes; stir everything and bake for another 15 minutes (the potatoes need to be tender and the chickpeas crispy)

The Kale

- In a large frying pan, heat the olive oil, add garlic and kale; cook them until the kale wilts; add 1 tsp. of lemon juice, salt, and pepper and cook them until the kale is soft;

Hummus

- Mix together all the ingredients (in a food processor); add water if necessary and season with salt and pepper;

- When you serve, add kale in two bowls, after that a layer of roasted vegetables, and a dressing of chickpeas and drizzle;

DESSERT AND OTHER VEGAN GOODIES

Protein bars

Ingredients (for 8 pieces)

→ 1 cup oats
→ ½ cup of dried fruits, chopped (raisins, apricots, cranberries etc.)
→ 1/8 cup nuts, chopped
→ 3 tbsp. hemp hearts
→ 1 small cup of soy protein
→ 2 tbsp. flax seeds
→ 1 banana
→ 3-4 tbsp. agave syrup
→ 1 tbsp. soy/almond milk
→ ½ cup of pitted dates
→ 30 grams of dark chocolate, melted

Instructions:

- Preheat the oven at a medium level;
- Combine in a bowl the oats, dried fruits, nuts, hemp and soy protein;
- Use a blender or a mixer to smooth banana, together with agave syrup, milk, and flax seeds;
- Combine the wet and the dry ingredients;
- Put the mixture on a baking sheet, in the baking tray; bake for 10-15 minutes and let them cool afterward;

- When it is cool, drizzle with chocolate (melted) and put it in the fridge until the chocolate is hard;

- Cut into pieces and keep it in the fridge.

Time needed: 20 minutes to prepare, 15 minutes to cook

Quick desserts:

1. fruits covered in chocolate:
   - 3 tbsp. coconut oil;
   - ½ cup of cocoa powder
   - 2 tbsp. maple syrup
   - A small bowl of chopped fruits (apples, strawberries, whatever you like)

Add all the ingredients in a saucepan (except the fruits); put them on a low heat and mix until it becomes soft and even; dip the fruits in the mixture, and let them cool down in the fridge for at least 15 minutes

2. Apple sandwich
   - An apple
   - Peanut butter
   - Bread
   - Cinnamon
   - chocolate

Peel the apple and slice it in whatever shape you want; take two slices of bread, spread peanut butter on the bread, add raisins, cinnamon, and chocolate; make a sandwich and cook it in the oven for 5-10 minutes, until the apple is soft;

3. Truffles
   - 1 cup almonds
   - ¼ cup cocoa
   - 2 tbsp. coconut oil
   - ½ tsp. vanilla
   - 10 dates, pitted
   - 2 tbsp. maple syrup

Mix all the ingredients in a blender/food processor; male balls from the mixture and keep it in the fridge for around 30 minutes; you can roll them in cocoa or coconut powder.

4. Cookies to go

- → 1cup oats
- → 1/2 cup packed raisins
- → 1/2cup coconut flour
- → 4 tbsp. maple syrup
- → 1cup peanut butter
- → 1 tsp vanilla

Combine all the ingredients in a bowl and make balls. To be kept in the fridge.

GOOD TO KNOW

Cooking measurements		Capacity	Weight
1 tablespoon (tbsp)	= 3 teaspoons (tsp)	15 ml	
	= 1/16 cup		
1 teaspoon		5 ml	100 grams
1 cup		237 ml	
4 cups		0.95 liter	
4.2 cups		1 liter	
2 tbsp	=1/8 cup		
4 tbsp	= ¼ cup		
8 tbsp	= ½ cup		
12 tbsp	= ¾ cup		
48 teaspoons	=1 cup		
16 tablespoons	= 1 cup		

The vegan food pyramid

The necessary amount of foods to be consumed daily in a vegan diet:

1. 2-4 cups of vegetables
2. 1-2 cups of fruits
3. 3-5 cups of whole grains
4. 1-2 cups dairy substitutes
5. 1-2 cup beans/seeds
6. 50 grams nuts
7. Fats and sweets (1/4 cups)

A quick list for a vegan kitchen

- → Nuts
- → Vegan milk
- → Agave syrup
- → Herbs and spices
- → Pasta
- → Vegetable stock
- → Beans
- → Dates
- → Quinoa
- → Nutritional Yeast
- → Applesauce
- → Flaxseeds
- → Vegan mayo

Thank You for choosing this book! If You liked it, please rate it on Amazon.com. I will be really appreciated!

Please check out my other veganism book on Amazon.com:

Veganism for Everyone – Step by Step Guide to Becoming a Healthy Vegan http://a.co/0tBS6a9

Made in the USA
San Bernardino, CA
28 April 2018